To Baby Panda

The Panda is Fat and Other Panda Haikus | written and illustrated
by Nolen Lee

Summary: A collection of haikus and illustrations featuring
the Punching Panda and his friend Red Panda.

Published by Punching Pandas, LLC.

First edition: March 2018
ISBN 978-0-9998235-0-7

punchingpandas.com

The Panda is **Fat**

and Other Panda Haikus

Written and illustrated by
Nolen Lee

Punching Pandas®

The panda is fat

The bamboo is on a hill

That is too much work

The meaning of life

What fulfills the inner self?

Inner self fulfilled

Birds of a feather

Will come and flock together

And poop on your head

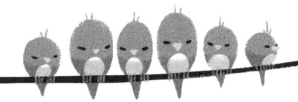

Patience breeds success

Good things come to those who wait

Any minute now

Fear is illusion

There's nothing to be scared of

Except black spiders

To be unselfish

Is to put others ahead

Can you hurry up?

Speaking slow is good

Listening first is better

Did you say something?

Trust takes time to build

But it is quickly broken

Broken, like my back

Wishing on a star

Can make all your dreams come true

But that's a planet

When life gets heavy

Look to others for support

Here, you carry it

To have contentment

Be thankful for what you have

You gonna eat that?

In competition

Rivals can bring out the best

I don't like this game

Always persevere

When we fall, we must rise up

I need assistance

What makes a good friend?

Those who always have your back

Or backside, same thing

29

A rested worker

Is a productive worker

I will go prepare

When work is busy

The week can fly by so fast

It's only Monday?

The mighty leader

Commands attention with words

And with free lunches

Achieving great heights

What does one need to reach this?

An elevator

If you never try

Then you will never succeed

You won't fail either

Risk is dangerous

But with risk comes great reward

A painful reward

44

Opportunity

Could be around the corner

So could misfortune

The path to success

One needs the drive and passion

And lots of coffee

Failure can help growth

Mistakes can lead to learning

Unless you're a klutz

I am ambitious

I will achieve all my goals

But after nap time

Baby, so precious

Baby, so pure and lovely

Baby, please, just sleep

Baby poops diaper

Baby gets brand new diaper

Baby poops again

Children's potential

No limits where they can go

Except there, no touch

A child full of life

Is like a flowing river

A dirty river

Baby is hard work

Baby needs a lot of care

Baby, I love you

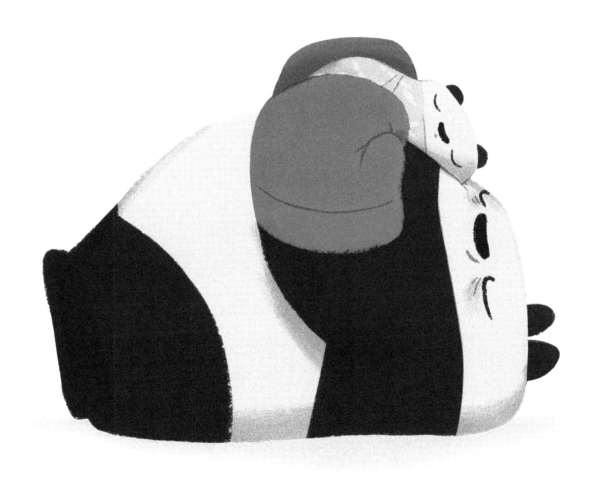

The night, so peaceful

The wind blows
       bugs chirp
           frogs croak

Night, please be quiet

An apple a day

Will keep the doctor away

Have some apples, doc

To complete a task

One can work hard or work smart

I choose working smart

Hurdles will appear

But panda will find a way

Panda needs ladder

Time will heal all wounds

Patience is good medicine

This might take a while

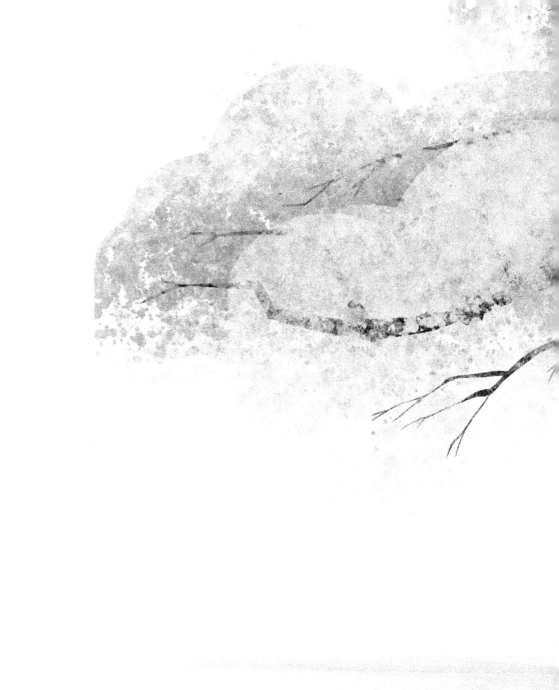

Art is expression

Drawing's really difficult

Art is frustration

Imagination

Makes the unseen visible

What the heck is that?

Singing, more than sound

It is the language of soul

Your soul is off-key

Cooking is an art

It's a painting of flavors

Tastes like abstract art

All art is unique

There is no right or wrong way

That looks terrible

86

Starting is easy

But finishing is what counts

Time to finish nap

Nolen Lee is the creator of Punching Pandas®
which he partly regrets. Originally from Portland,
Oregon, he discovered drawing at a young age and
decided to pursue his passion by enrolling six years
of his life into engineering. He later came to his
senses and has been playing catch up ever since.
He lives in the Seattle area where the traffic is bad
and the weather is crummy. He also managed to get
married somehow and reproduce.

CPSIA information can be obtained
at www.ICGtesting.com
Printed in the USA
LVHW051139061119
636517LV00006B/229/P

9 780999 823507